Deliberate Dissolution

Moving through divorce without taking your baggage

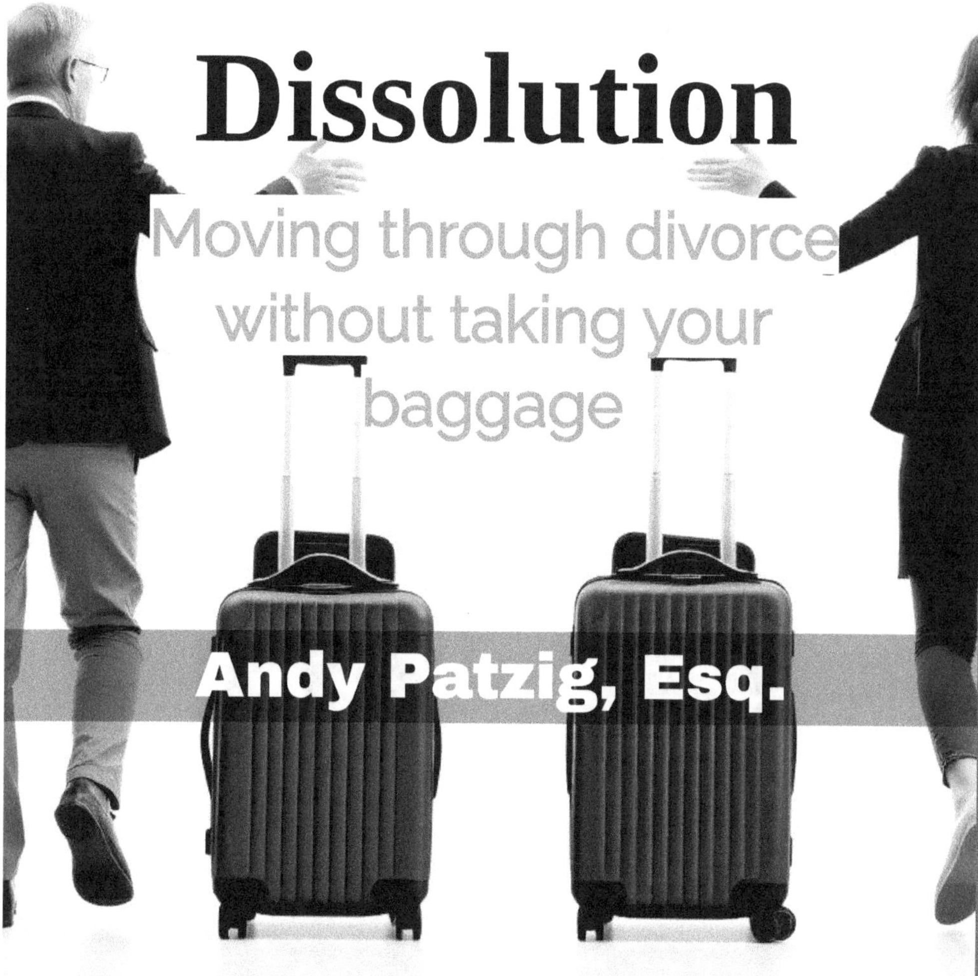

Andy Patzig, Esq.

Table Of Contents

Section 1: Introduction - Establishing a Foundation for Successful Co-Parenting

The dissolution of a marriage is a legally complex process. It is often full of emotional turmoil. When children are involved, the stakes are significantly higher. Navigating this terrain requires a strategic approach, one that prioritizes the " best interests of the child", as the court would say. If you are facing this situation, you seek to minimize conflict. You want to establish a stable environment for your children.

As a Guardian ad litem (GAL) in the Virginia court's I have seen a lot of examples of parents who tried to avoid bringing their children into their personal issues and I have seen what happens when parents put their own interests before those of the children. I have personally experienced a child who was afraid to make a decision about where he wanted to live because he was so worried that one of his parents would be disappointed with him. I had to work with this child to empower them to speak to me about their concerns so I could advocate for their best interests. It's wonderful that we have a GAL program in Virginia but it's also unfortunate that we need them in divorces.

Deliberate Dissolution of Divorce

Choosing to read this guide clearly indicates that you are prepared and motivated to initiate a positive change in your current situation. This guide provides a warm and supportive framework for the concept of "Deliberate Dissolution." It presents a thoughtful and compassionate approach to separating while ensuring that respect and kindness remain at the forefront of this process. Throughout this journey, the well-being and emotional health of your children are paramount and will always be the top priorities as you navigate these changes. Additionally, you can approach this transition with confidence, knowing that the strategies outlined in this guide are not only practical but also legally sound, which will offer you peace of mind as you work through this significant life change.

Deliberate Dissolution of Divorce

My own experience with marital dissolution was challenging. My divorce had it's own complexities and resolutions that are unique from yours in that we are different people with different life experiences. I understand the emotional and legal complexities involved in divorce having been involved in many divorces and custody hearings for my clients. As an attorney, I saw firsthand the adversarial nature of many divorces. The impact on the children involved was often devastating. This led me to explore alternative dispute resolution methods. I focused on collaborative law, specifically Deliberate Dissolution. I developed a unique step-by-step process for achieving a more amicable separation. This is detailed in this guide.

This process will help you achieve the following:

- Establish effective communication with your former spouse.
- Create a stable and predictable environment for your children.
- Negotiate mutually agreeable solutions regarding custody and support.
- Ensure the best interests of your children remain paramount.
- Establish a new family dynamic based on cooperation.

Deliberate Dissolution of Divorce

This is not merely about surviving divorce; it's about establishing a strong framework for a successful and fulfilling future. Your children's well-being will be safeguarded and prioritized throughout this process. A cooperative and supportive environment will greatly facilitate healing, growth, and positive development for everyone involved.

My legal expertise provides me with unique qualifications. I have litigated countless family law cases. I have also mediated numerous settlements. I have witnessed the destructive nature of acrimonious divorces. I've also seen the positive outcomes of collaborative approaches. This experience informs every aspect of this guide. As an attorney, I find it incredibly rewarding to see parents come together for the children. I once had a divorced couple who were back in court regarding custody and visitation. One of the children was very gifted in the arts. It took a little time and work but eventually the parents were able to put the child's talent before their own desires and the mother was able to relocate with the children to a new community that embraced the child's artistic gifts and encouraged their growth.

Section 2: The Myths - Debunking Misconceptions About Divorce and Child Custody

Prevailing societal narratives about divorce frequently misrepresent its realities, especially regarding the impact it has on children. These narratives are often steeped in inaccuracies and oversimplifications, perpetuating myths that can amplify the emotional and social challenges families face during what is already a difficult and transformative period. For instance, many people assume that divorce universally leads to negative outcomes for children, failing to account for the nuances of individual family dynamics and the potential benefits of removing children from high-conflict environments. I have personally witnessed a case where one parent had a substance abuse issue which affected the whole family.

By proceeding with the divorce the toxic environment which had existed, no longer overshadowed the child and they were able to finally feel a sense of wellness and relief.

Such misconceptions not only distort public understanding but can also influence legal decisions, social attitudes, and the resources available to families in transition. It is crucial to address these myths from a legal and psychological standpoint, as this can provide a more balanced and evidence-based perspective on how divorce affects children. By dispelling these misconceptions, we can empower families with accurate information, reduce stigma, and foster a more supportive and understanding environment for those navigating the complexities of divorce. This approach encourages a shift in focus—from seeing divorce solely as a source of harm to recognizing it as an opportunity for growth, healing, and healthier family dynamics when managed thoughtfully.

Myth #1: Divorce inevitably results in irreparable harm to children.

Reality: While divorce can present numerous challenges for children, it is essential to recognize that it is not inherently damaging to their well-being. The most critical determining factor in this situation is the level of inter-parental conflict experienced during and after the divorce process. High levels of conflict between parents can substantially increase the risk of negative emotional and psychological outcomes for children involved. In contrast, the practice of Deliberate Dissolution actively seeks to minimize conflict between parents. This approach prioritizes the emotional well-being of the child above all else, ensuring that their needs and feelings are taken into account throughout the transition.

Furthermore, this method aligns effectively with the established legal principle that emphasizes acting in the "best interests of the child," ensuring that their welfare remains at the forefront of any decisions made during the divorce.

The actual harm that can be inflicted on children within the bounds of a marriage has the potential to be devastating and irreparably harming to the children. I have represented a child who tested positive for chrystal meth because their father road around smoking meth while the 12 year old was in the car. The damage done by a parent far outweighs the difficulties of divorcing parents and two households. Children are resilient but should be protected from the harm that some parents inflict.

Myth #2: Effective co-parenting requires a close, amicable relationship between former spouses.

Reality: Cordiality is undeniably beneficial in any relationship. However, effective co-parenting primarily necessitates a strong commitment to cooperation between the parents. This commitment is ultimately in service of meeting and prioritizing the children's needs. Deliberate Dissolution offers a structured framework that fosters this essential cooperation. It emphasizes the importance of respectful communication and collaborative joint decision-making. This approach remains crucial, regardless of the personal feelings or tensions that may exist between the parties involved. By focusing on the well-being of the children, parents can work together more effectively.

Myth #3: Divorce signifies the termination of the family unit.

Reality: Divorce legally dissolves the marital relationship. It does not, however, dissolve the familial bonds between parents and children. Deliberate Dissolution facilitates the restructuring of the family. It allows both parents to remain actively involved in their children's lives. This is consistent with legal precedents that uphold the importance of both parents in a child's upbringing.

The legal industry, in some ways, contributes to these misconceptions. An adversarial approach can incentivize conflict. This can be detrimental to the well-being of all parties. Especially the children. My process offers a different approach. It emphasizes collaboration and mutually beneficial outcomes. It aligns with the principles of collaborative law and alternative dispute resolution.

Myth #4. Divorce Means "Failure".

Reality: Divorce is not a failure but rather a decision to prioritize the well-being of individuals and families. Staying in a toxic or unfulfilling marriage can sometimes cause more harm than choosing to part ways. Divorce is better viewed as a step toward personal growth and a healthier future for everyone involved.

Myth #5. Mothers Always Get Custody of the Children.

Reality: While this may have been true in the past under Virginia's "Tender Years Doctrine", modern family courts prioritize the best interests of the child, which doesn't necessarily mean awarding custody to the mother. Today, there is a growing recognition of the importance of both parents being involved, and shared or joint custody arrangements are increasingly common. The best interest factors in Virginia consist of ten factors that the court must consider when deciding on custody and/or visitation.

Myth #6. Divorce is Always Contentious.

Reality: Not all divorces are adversarial. Many couples resolve their differences amicably through mediation or collaborative divorce processes. These approaches emphasize communication and compromise, allowing couples to separate without hostility and create mutually beneficial agreements.

Myth #7. Divorce Is Always Expensive.

Reality: While some divorces can be costly, this largely depends on the complexity of the case and the willingness of both parties to cooperate. Mediation and uncontested divorces are typically far less expensive than litigation. Additionally, financial planning and open dialogue can help mitigate costs.

Myth #8. Divorced People Are Doomed to Be Alone.

Reality: Many people find happiness and successful relationships after divorce. In fact, for some, leaving an unhealthy or incompatible marriage allows them to rediscover themselves and build stronger relationships in the future. Divorce can be an opportunity for personal growth and a fresh start. My current wife told me years ago, the first marriage is often like the first pancake. It often doesn't come out right and their is no shame in throwing it out.

I once had a new client and while speaking with her during her initial consultation she said to me "I don't have it that bad, some people are much worse off than me." My response to her was that she was looking at it backwards, the question should be do other marriages have it better than you. If the answer is yes and your spouse is not willing to make the changes necessary in your relationship to achieve happiness, you owe it to yourself to get out of that marriage and start the next chapter.

Myth #9. Divorce Is Always a "Last Resort".

Reality: While some couples try counseling and other interventions before divorcing, others may decide early on that their marriage is no longer viable or healthy. Divorce is a personal decision, and there is no universal "right way" to approach it.

Myth #10. Property and Finances Are Always Split 50/50.

Reality: The division of property and finances depends on the laws of the specific jurisdiction and the unique circumstances of the marriage. Some states follow "community property" rules (equal division), while others, like Virginia, follow "equitable distribution" principles, which aim for fairness rather than strict equality.

Myth #11. It's Better to Stay in a Bad Marriage for the Kids.

Reality: Children frequently experience more significant negative impacts from ongoing parental conflict than they do from the process of divorce itself. A calm and cooperative co-parenting arrangement after divorce tends to be much healthier for children compared to a household filled with tension and hostility.

Myth #12. Divorce Is the End of Financial Security.

Reality: While divorce can create financial challenges, it doesn't have to lead to ruin. Careful planning, budgeting, and rebuilding financial independence can help individuals regain stability. Additionally, courts often ensure that spousal support (alimony) and child support are awarded when necessary to protect vulnerable parties.

Section 3: Can Divorce Ever Be Amicable and Friendly?

Yes, divorce can absolutely be amicable and friendly, though it requires effort, mutual respect, and a shared commitment to handling the process in a constructive way. While divorce is often associated with conflict and animosity, many couples successfully navigate the end of their marriage in a way that prioritizes cooperation, communication, and the well-being of everyone involved. This type of divorce can be referred to as a "Deliberate Dissolution" or an amicable divorce. Below, we'll explore how and why divorce can be friendly, as well as strategies to achieve it.

Why divorce can be amicable and what can you do to make the entire situation less hostile and contentious.

1. A Shared Goal of Peaceful Resolution: Some couples recognize that their relationship is no longer working but want to part ways in a respectful and dignified manner. They may prioritize maintaining a positive dynamic, especially if children are involved.
2. Minimized Emotional and Financial Costs: A contentious divorce can be emotionally draining and financially expensive. Many couples prefer to avoid courtroom battles and instead work together to reach agreements that benefit both parties.
3. Focus on Co-Parenting: When children are involved, amicable divorces are often motivated by the desire to create a stable, supportive co-parenting relationship and minimize the impact on the children.

4. Mutual Respect and Understanding: If both parties respect each other and agree that ending the marriage is the best decision, it creates a foundation for a friendlier separation.

How to Achieve an Amicable Divorce

Section 1: Introduction - Establishing a Foundation for Successful Co-Parenting

1. **Choose Mediation or Collaborative Divorce Over Litigation**

   Litigation often creates an adversarial environment, while mediation and collaborative divorce emphasize finding solutions together. These approaches allow couples to work with neutral professionals (like mediators or collaborative attorneys) to resolve disputes peacefully.

2. **Prioritize Open and Honest Communication**

   Clear and respectful communication is key to avoiding misunderstandings and unnecessary conflict. Both parties should be transparent about their needs, concerns, and expectations.

3. **Focus on Common Goals**

   Whether it's ensuring the well-being of children, dividing assets fairly, or maintaining a positive relationship, identifying shared goals can help keep the process constructive.

4. **Separate Emotions from Decision-Making**

Divorce is emotional, but it's important to approach decisions with a practical mindset. Seeking support from therapists or counselors can help both parties process feelings without letting them derail the divorce process.

5. **Establish Clear Boundaries**

   An amicable divorce doesn't mean you have to be best friends. Setting healthy boundaries allows both parties to move forward respectfully while maintaining their independence.

6. **Keep Children's Best Interests at Heart**

   If children are involved, focusing on their needs can motivate both parties to cooperate and compromise. Shielding children from conflict and working together as co-parents is critical.

7. **Use Neutral Professionals**

   Engaging financial advisors, child specialists, or marriage-friendly divorce coaches can help guide the process objectively and reduce tension.

8. **Avoid Blame and Finger-Pointing**

   Focusing on assigning blame can make the divorce process more contentious. Instead, approach the situation as a shared decision to move forward in a healthier way.

Examples of Amicable Divorce

- Deliberate Dissolution: Popularized by celebrities like Gwyneth Paltrow and Chris Martin, this concept emphasizes ending the relationship with mutual respect and a focus on personal growth rather than resentment.
- Collaborative Co-Parenting: Many divorced couples successfully maintain positive relationships as co-parents, working together to raise their children in a supportive and unified way, even after separating.

Friendships Post-Divorce:

Some couples remain friends after divorce, maintaining a cordial and sometimes even close relationship while moving on with their individual lives.

Benefits of an Amicable Divorce

1. Reduced Stress: An amicable divorce eliminates much of the anxiety, hostility, and emotional toll associated with contentious separations.
2. Faster Resolution: Cooperative divorces are often resolved more quickly than litigated ones, as both parties are motivated to find solutions rather than argue.
3. Lower Costs: With fewer legal disputes, amicable divorces tend to cost significantly less than court battles.
4. Healthier Relationships Post-Divorce: Maintaining a positive dynamic sets the stage for future cooperation, especially if you'll continue to co-parent or interact.

5. Better Outcomes for Children: Children benefit significantly when parents handle divorce respectfully and avoid exposing them to conflict.

Final Thoughts

While not every divorce can be amicable (especially if there's a history of abuse, betrayal, or extreme conflict), many couples find that they can separate in a friendly and respectful manner when both parties are committed to the process. An amicable divorce requires communication, compromise, and emotional maturity, but it can pave the way for a healthier and more harmonious future for everyone involved.

Section 4: The Mechanics - A Legal Blueprint for Deliberate Dissolution

This section thoroughly outlines the procedural steps necessary for successfully achieving a Deliberate Dissolution. It provides a legally sound and robust framework for effectively navigating the complexities that often accompany divorce, all while prioritizing the welfare and best interests of your children. Each step involved in this process is explained in detail below to ensure clarity and understanding

Step 1: Unequivocal Commitment to the Best Interests of the Child.

The essence of Deliberate Dissolution is deeply rooted in this important idea. This concept is also a fundamental principle in family law. It emphasizes the necessity of prioritizing your children's needs above any personal feelings or emotions you may still harbor for your former spouse. This approach encourages individuals to focus on what is best for their children during a challenging time, ensuring that their well-being remains at the forefront of any decisions made.

- Action: Before each interaction with your ex-spouse, reaffirm this commitment. Ensure your actions align with this principle.
- Resources: Familiarize yourself with your jurisdiction's legal standards regarding the "best interests of the child." Consult with a family law attorney to understand your rights and responsibilities. The book "Putting Children First" by JoAnne Pedro-Carroll is still relevant here.
- Benefit: This creates a child-centric approach to decision-making, which not only protects their well-being but also actively fosters their healthy development and growth.

Results:

Your children will exhibit greater emotional stability. They will demonstrate increased resilience. You will be in a stronger legal position should any disputes arise.

Step 2: Negotiate and Execute a Comprehensive Co-Parenting Agreement.

Negotiating and executing a comprehensive co-parenting agreement is a crucial step for parents who are separating or divorcing but want to ensure the best possible environment for their children. This process requires careful planning, effective communication, and a focus on the child's well-being. Here's a comprehensive guide on how to negotiate and execute a co-parenting agreement:

1. Understanding the Essential Components

A comprehensive co-parenting agreement should include several key elements to ensure clarity and minimize potential conflicts

1. Parenting Time and Custody Schedule: This is one of the most critical components, outlining the division of parenting time, including specific days and times for each parent, as well as holiday and vacation schedules.
2. Decision-Making Authority: Specify how decisions regarding the child's education, health care, and other significant matters will be made.
3. Communication Plan: Establish a clear communication plan for effective co-parenting, including how parents will communicate about the child's needs and any schedule changes.

4. Dispute Resolution Mechanisms: Include methods for resolving disagreements, such as mediation or arbitration, to avoid litigation.
5. Financial Responsibilities: Outline the financial obligations of each parent, including child support, medical expenses, and costs related to extracurricular activities.
6. Transportation Arrangements: Detail pick-up and drop-off arrangements to ensure smooth transitions between households.

7. Flexibility and Modifications: Allow for flexibility to accommodate changes in circumstances and outline the process for making modifications to the agreement.
8. Child-Centered Focus: Prioritize the best interests of the child in all decisions and arrangements.

2. Effective Communication Strategies

To negotiate with successfully, employ these communication strategies

1. Clear and Respectful Communication: Maintain clear, concise, and respectful communication to reduce misunderstandings and promote cooperation.
2. Use "I" Statements: Express feelings and needs without blaming the other parent to manage emotions and reduce defensiveness.
3. Active Listening: Practice active listening to understand each other's perspectives better.
4. Establish Boundaries: Clearly define acceptable behaviors and communication times to maintain structured and respectful interactions.

5. Utilize Written Communication: Use written communication for complex issues or when emotions are high to ensure clarity and maintain a record of discussions.
6. Prioritize Child-Centered Communication: Keep the focus on the child's needs and well-being to align both parents' efforts towards a common goal.

3. Negotiation Techniques

Employ these negotiation techniques to reach a mutually beneficial agreement

1. Cooperative Approach: Adopt a cooperative mindset, working together towards shared parenting goals.
2. Create a Parenting Plan: Develop a detailed parenting plan that outlines responsibilities, schedules, and decision-making processes.
3. Seek Mediation When Necessary: Consider involving a neutral third party to facilitate discussions and help resolve conflicts.
4. Discuss and Align on Goals: Regularly discuss and align on parenting goals and values to ensure both parents are on the same page.
5. Problem-Solving Techniques: Use structured problem-solving techniques to address disagreements effectively.

4. Utilizing Professional Support and Resources

Take advantage of available resources and professional support to navigate the process.

1. Family Law Attorneys: Consult with family law attorneys to understand legal requirements and implications.
2. Mediators: Consider mediation as an alternative to litigation for resolving disputes and negotiating agreements.
3. Collaborative Divorce Professionals: Explore collaborative divorce options, which involve working with mental health and financial experts.
4. Co-Parenting Therapists: Engage in co-parenting therapy to improve communication and cooperation.
5. Parenting Coordinators: Utilize parenting coordinators to facilitate negotiations and resolve disputes.

6. Co-Parenting Apps and Tools: Use digital tools like OurFamilyWizard or Talking Parents to facilitate communication and organization.
7. Parenting Classes and Workshops: Attend parenting classes or workshops to gain valuable insights and strategies.
8. Financial Advisors: Consult financial advisors for issues related to child support and financial planning.

5. Addressing Potential Conflicts and Future Modifications

Implement strategies to manage conflicts and make future modifications.

1. Early Intervention: Address conflicts as soon as they arise to prevent escalation.
2. Understanding Motivations: Uncover underlying motivations to find common ground and address root causes of conflict.
3. Flexibility in Agreements: Ensure the agreement is flexible enough to accommodate changes in circumstances.
4. Regular Reviews: Set up regular reviews and updates to the agreement as needed.
5. Professional Support: Engage mediators or family therapists to provide neutral ground for discussions and facilitate modifications.

6. Legal Considerations

Be aware of legal requirements and considerations. Understand how the process works in your specific state. Their is a lot of variety in the way different states structure their court system and how formal/informal the process is.

1. Uniform Child-Custody Jurisdiction and Enforcement Act (UCCJEA): Understand how this act affects interstate custody cases.
2. State-Specific Jurisdiction Rules: Be aware of jurisdiction rules specific to your state.
3. Inter-Jurisdictional Enforcement: Consider how the agreement will be enforced across different legal jurisdictions.
4. Legal Requirements: Ensure the agreement complies with state-specific laws and guidelines and is in the best interest of the child.

7. Best Practices for Child-Centered Agreements

Implement these best practices to create a child-centered agreement

1. Prioritize the Child's Needs: Focus on creating a stable and supportive environment for the child.
2. Consistency and Stability: Maintain consistent routines across both households.
3. Effective Communication: Establish clear guidelines for communication between parents.
4. Flexibility and Adaptability: Be open to modifying the arrangement as necessary.
5. Decision-Making Protocols: Clearly outline how decisions regarding the child will be made.
6. Conflict Resolution Mechanisms: Establish clear methods for resolving disagreements.

7. Incorporate Technology: Utilize technology to facilitate communication and coordination.
8. Involve Children Appropriately: When appropriate, involve children in the planning process in an age-appropriate manner.
9. Regular Review and Adjustment: Regularly review and update the co-parenting agreement to reflect changes in circumstances.

By following these comprehensive steps and best practices, parents can negotiate and execute a co-parenting agreement that prioritizes their child's well-being, minimizes conflicts, and provides a stable foundation for effective co-parenting.

- Action: Engage in good-faith negotiations with your ex-spouse. Consider mediation if direct communication proves difficult.
- Resources: Utilize online resources, such as OurFamilyWizard and CoParently. These provide templates and tools for drafting co-parenting agreements. Consult with your attorney to ensure the agreement is legally sound and enforceable.
- Benefit: This provides a clear and predictable framework for co-parenting. This minimizes ambiguity and potential conflict.

Results:
You will experience fewer disputes with your ex-spouse regarding logistical matters. Your children will benefit from the stability and predictability the agreement provides.

Step 4: Establish and Maintain Respectful Communication.

Effective communication is essential for successful co-parenting. This requires a commitment to respectful dialogue. Even when disagreements arise. There are some great tools on the market which will allow parents to communicate without relying on texting or emails. OurFamilyWizard is one such tool and has a plethora of tools, it even has a tone monitor to let you know if your language may be a bit to strong. TalkingParents is another good but lower priced tool to facilitate communications. I would be remise if I didn't mention Fayr which is the one Gwyneth Paltrow is involved in, since she is an advocate for Deliberate Dissolution.

- Action: Employ active listening techniques. Utilize "I" statements to express your needs and concerns. Refrain from accusatory or inflammatory language.
- Resources: Review materials on non-violent communication. Consult with a therapist or counselor to develop effective communication strategies. The book "Difficult Conversations" by Douglas Stone, Bruce Patton, and Sheila Heen is still a good resource.
- Benefit: This facilitates constructive dialogue. It allows for the amicable resolution of disputes. It models healthy communication for your children.

Results:

You will find it easier to address sensitive issues with your ex-spouse. You will avoid unnecessary escalation of conflict.

Step 5: Maintain a Consistent and Predictable Environment for Your Children.

Divorce can be a challenging and disruptive time for families, particularly for children who may struggle with the changes in their lives. However, by focusing on creating a consistent and predictable environment, parents can significantly mitigate the negative impacts of divorce on their children's well-being. This comprehensive guide will explore effective strategies to maintain stability during this transitional period.

Understanding the Importance of Consistency

Before delving into practical strategies, it's crucial to understand why consistency is so vital for children during divorce. Research has shown that a stable environment can have profound positive effects on children's long-term emotional and psychological well-being. Consistency provides children with a sense of security and normalcy during a time of significant change, helping them to better cope with the stress and uncertainty of divorce.

Challenges in Maintaining Consistency

Parents often face several challenges when trying to maintain a stable environment during divorce:

1. Emotional Turmoil: The stress and emotional upheaval of divorce can make it difficult for parents to focus on their children's needs.
2. Communication Breakdown: Effective co-parenting requires good communication, which can be challenging during divorce.
3. Logistical Complexities: Managing separate households and coordinating schedules can lead to inconsistencies.
4. Financial Strain: Divorce often brings financial challenges that can impact the resources available for children's activities and needs.

Despite these challenges, there are several strategies that parents can employ to create a more consistent and predictable environment for their children.

Practical Strategies for Creating Consistency

1. Establish Clear Routines and Schedules

Creating and maintaining consistent daily routines is crucial for providing children with a sense of stability:

- Set specific times for meals, homework, bedtime, and other daily activities.
- Use visual aids like calendars or charts to help children understand and follow routines.
- Maintain similar routines across both households when possible to reduce confusion and anxiety.

2. Develop a Comprehensive Co-Parenting Plan

A well-thought-out co-parenting plan can significantly reduce conflicts and provide predictability:

- Create a detailed schedule for visitation, holidays, and important events.
- Agree on rules and expectations for both households to maintain consistency.
- Use co-parenting apps or shared calendars to keep both parents informed and aligned.

3. Prioritize Open and Respectful Communication

Effective communication between co-parents is essential for maintaining a stable environment:

- Focus on child-related issues and avoid personal conflicts when communicating.
- Use neutral language and a business-like tone in all interactions.
- Consider using a mediator or family therapist to facilitate communication if needed.

4. Maintain Consistent Rules and Discipline

Consistency in rules and discipline across both households helps children feel secure:

- Agree on major rules and consequences with your co-parent.
- Follow through with promised consequences and rewards consistently.
- Avoid undermining the other parent's authority or rules.

5. Create a Supportive Emotional Environment

Children need emotional support to navigate the challenges of divorce:

- Encourage open expression of feelings and provide a safe space for children to share their concerns.
- Reassure children that both parents love them and that the divorce is not their fault.
- Consider professional counseling or support groups for children to help them process their emotions.

6. Utilize Professional Resources and Support

Don't hesitate to seek professional help when needed:

- Engage with family therapists or counselors specializing in divorce.
- Participate in co-parenting education programs to learn effective strategies.
- Consult with legal professionals to ensure fair and child-focused arrangements.

7. Be Flexible and Cooperative

While consistency is important, flexibility is also necessary:

- Be willing to adjust plans when unexpected situations arise.
- Cooperate with your co-parent to accommodate special events or changes in circumstances.
- Model positive problem-solving skills for your children.

Long-Term Benefits of Consistency

Maintaining a consistent environment during and after divorce can have significant long-term benefits for children:

- Emotional Stability: Children are less likely to develop mood disorders and have better emotional regulation.
- Academic Success: A stable home environment supports better focus and academic achievement.
- Healthy Social Relationships: Consistency fosters better social skills and the ability to form healthy relationships.
- Reduced Risk Behaviors: Children are less likely to engage in substance abuse or other risky behaviors.
- Overall Well-Being: Long-term mental health outcomes are generally more positive for children who experience stability during divorce.

Conclusion

Divorce is undoubtedly a challenging time for families, but by prioritizing consistency and predictability, parents can significantly mitigate its negative impacts on their children. By establishing clear routines, maintaining open communication, and utilizing available resources, parents can create a stable environment that supports their children's emotional and psychological well-being. Remember that consistency doesn't mean rigidity – flexibility and cooperation are also key components of successful co-parenting. With dedication and effort, parents can help their children navigate the challenges of divorce and emerge as resilient, well-adjusted individuals.

- Action: Collaborate with your ex-spouse to establish similar expectations regarding bedtime, meals, homework, and disciplinary measures.
- Resources: Utilize shared online calendars and apps, such as 2Houses and Cozi Family Organizer. These help coordinate schedules and maintain consistency.
- Benefit: This provides a sense of stability and security for your children. This minimizes confusion and promotes their emotional adjustment.
- Results: Your children will exhibit improved behavior and adaptability. They will transition more easily between households.

Step 6: Establish a Strong Support Network.

Divorce is a challenging and transformative phase in life, often accompanied by emotional, practical, and legal complexities. Establishing a robust support network during this time can significantly impact one's ability to navigate the process effectively and emerge stronger on the other side. Here's a comprehensive guide on how to build a strong support network during divorce:

Understanding the Importance of a Support Network

Before diving into the strategies for building a support network, it's crucial to understand why it's so important:

1. Emotional Resilience: A strong support network can enhance confidence and resilience, helping individuals manage the emotional turmoil associated with divorce.
2. Safe Space for Sharing: Support groups provide a safe and nurturing environment where individuals can share their experiences, emotions, and challenges without fear of judgment.
3. Practical and Legal Assistance: A well-rounded support system can offer not only emotional but also practical and legal assistance, helping with navigating legal processes, financial planning, and addressing housing concerns.

4. Sense of Community: Joining a divorce support group can provide solace, understanding, and a sense of community, helping individuals feel less alone during this difficult time.

5. Long-term Benefits: The support system cultivated during divorce can remain valuable in the years to come, providing ongoing emotional and practical support as individuals adjust to their new lives.

Strategies for Building a Strong Support Network

1. Identify Your Needs

Before seeking support, it's essential to identify the types of support you need. This may include:

- Emotional support
- Practical assistance (e.g., childcare, household management)
- Legal advice
- Financial guidance

Understanding your specific needs will help you target the right resources and individuals for your support network.

2. Reach Out to Family and Friends

Family and friends can be a crucial part of your support network:

- Communicate your needs clearly to them.
- Be open about your situation and how they can help.
- Set boundaries about what kind of support is helpful and what isn't.

Remember, it's okay to ask for help. Many people want to support you but may not know how unless you tell them.

3. Join Support Groups

Support groups can be an invaluable resource during divorce:

- Online Support Groups: Platforms like Circles, DailyStrength, and DivorceCare offer online support groups that provide flexibility and accessibility.
- Local Support Groups: Look for local divorce support groups in your community, often hosted by churches, community centers, or mental health clinics.
- Specialized Groups: Consider joining groups that cater to specific needs, such as groups for parents or those focused on particular demographics.

4. Seek Professional Help

Professional support can provide specialized guidance:

- Therapists and Counselors: Individual therapy can offer personalized support and coping strategies.
- Legal Advisors: A divorce attorney can help you understand your legal rights and navigate the complexities of the divorce process.
- Consider consulting a Certified Divorce Financial Analyst (CDFA) to help with financial planning during and after divorce.

5. Utilize Online Resources

The digital world offers numerous resources for support:

- Online Forums: Participate in online forums where you can ask questions, share experiences, and receive advice from peers.
- Virtual Support Groups: Join virtual support groups that offer regular meetings and discussions.
- Educational Workshops: Attend online workshops or webinars that provide information on various aspects of divorce.

6. Engage in Self-Care Activities

While building your external support network, don't forget to take care of yourself:

- Engage in activities that promote mental well-being, such as exercise, meditation, and hobbies.
- Join classes or groups related to your interests, which can help you meet new people and maintain a sense of normalcy.

7. Develop Effective Communication Strategies

As you build your support network, it's crucial to communicate effectively:

- Practice active listening when interacting with your support network.
- Use "I" statements to express your feelings without blaming others.
- Avoid contentious topics and absolute language when discussing your divorce.

8. Overcome Challenges in Building Support

Building a support network during divorce can come with challenges:

• Emotional Vulnerability: Combat feelings of isolation by actively reaching out to others and joining support groups.

• Fear of Judgment: Be clear about your needs and set boundaries with your support network to avoid feeling judged

. • Practical Barriers: Utilize technology to stay connected with distant friends and family, and consider online support options

Conclusion

Establishing a strong support network during divorce is not just beneficial but essential for navigating this challenging life transition. By actively seeking out diverse sources of support - from friends and family to professional resources and support groups - you can create a robust network that provides emotional comfort, practical assistance, and valuable guidance. Remember, it's okay to ask for help, and doing so can significantly ease the transition into post-divorce life. With the right support, you can emerge from this process stronger and more self-assured than you may have thought possible

- Action: Seek support from trusted friends, family members, or mental health professionals.

Consider joining a support group for divorced parents.

- Resources: Explore online forums and communities for divorced individuals. Consult with a therapist specializing in divorce and co-parenting.
- Benefit: This provides emotional support and practical guidance. It helps you navigate the challenges of co-parenting.
- Results: You will feel less isolated and better equipped to manage stress. You will make more informed decisions.

Section 4: Maintenance - Addressing Potential Challenges to Co-Parenting

Addressing potential challenges to co-parenting during and after divorce is crucial for maintaining a healthy environment for children and fostering a cooperative relationship between parents. Based on the research provided, here's a comprehensive guide on how to address these challenges:

1. Effective Communication Strategies

Communication is the cornerstone of successful co-parenting. To address this challenge:

1. Practice Effective Communication Skills: Focus on controlling emotions and scheduling regular co-parenting phone calls to address issues systematically
2. Limit Personal Topics: Keep conversations centered on the child's needs, avoiding unrelated personal matters that could lead to conflict
3. Use "I" Statements: Express feelings without blaming the other parent to reduce defensiveness and promote constructive dialogue.
4. Communicate Through Texts and Emails: This method helps co-parents stay focused on parenting-related communication and avoid face-to-face confrontations that might escalate into conflicts

5. Maintain Respectful Communication: Keep communication clear, concise, and respectful. Avoid using derogatory language or making accusations

2. Conflict Resolution Techniques

Conflicts are inevitable, but they can be managed effectively:

1. Empathy and Cooperative Mindset: Practice empathy towards each other to understand different perspectives and reduce conflicts
2. Advanced Conflict Resolution Strategies: Set clear boundaries, maintain open communication, and focus on the child's best interests.
3. Professional Support and Mediation: Seek professional support through therapy, mediation, or co-parenting classes to gain tools and strategies for managing conflicts
4. Strategic and Social-Psychological Problem Solving: Utilize logical and structured approaches to resolving issues, while also focusing on understanding the emotional and relational aspects of conflicts

3. Addressing Emotional Challenges

Emotional challenges can significantly impact co-parenting relationships:

1. Manage Emotional Triggers and Resentment: Recognize and address ongoing resentment and emotional triggers that can hinder cooperative co-parenting.
2. Provide Emotional Support to Children: Ensure children receive adequate emotional support during the transition, even if parents are struggling with their own emotional challenges.
3. Utilize Therapeutic Techniques: Consider play therapy for younger children to help them express emotions in a safe and supportive environment
4. Teach Relaxation and Mindfulness: Help children manage their emotions and reduce stress through relaxation techniques and mindfulness exercises.

4. Navigating Parenting Decisions and Consistency

Disagreements on parenting decisions can create challenges:

1. Establish Clear Boundaries and Guidelines: Use a shared calendar or schedule regular check-ins to avoid misunderstandings
2. Maintain Consistency: Be consistent in communication and make an effort to cooperate with each other to enhance the co-parenting relationship.
3. Focus on Child-Centered Decisions: Keep the focus on the children's well-being when making decisions, ensuring their needs are prioritized

5. Legal and Financial Considerations

Legal and financial issues can add stress to co-parenting relationships:

1. Understand Legal and Custody Arrangements: Familiarize yourself with legal agreements regarding custody and visitation to ensure clarity about rights and responsibilities
2. Address Financial Strain: Openly discuss and agree on financial responsibilities to minimize conflicts related to financial matters
3. Utilize Resources: Seek assistance from the Friend of the Court office for creating parenting time schedules and resolving disputes

6. Adapting to New Family Dynamics

Adjusting to new family structures can be challenging:

1. Navigate New Relationships: Address the introduction of new partners into the family dynamic with sensitivity and open communication.
2. Maintain Flexibility: Be flexible with schedules and parenting plans to accommodate changing needs of children and parents
3. Create a Supportive Environment: Consider attending family events together and celebrating milestones as a family unit when possible, to help children feel loved and supported by both parents.

By implementing these strategies, co-parents can effectively address the potential challenges that arise during and after divorce. Remember that successful co-parenting is an ongoing process that requires patience, commitment, and a willingness to put the children's needs first. With time and effort, co-parents can create a stable, supportive environment that promotes the well-being of their children.

Potential Roadblock #1: Disagreements Regarding Parental Decision-Making.

Differing parenting philosophies can often lead to significant conflict between parents. This is especially true when it comes to making important decisions about the children's upbringing and the values they will instill in them.

Prevention:

- Clearly Define Decision-Making Authority: Your co-parenting agreement should clearly delineate decision-making responsibilities. This should cover areas such as education, healthcare, and religious upbringing.
- Consult with Experts: When facing complex decisions, seek guidance from relevant professionals. These can be educators, medical practitioners, or therapists.
- Utilize Mediation: If disagreements persist, engage a neutral third-party mediator. This will facilitate constructive dialogue and help you reach a mutually agreeable resolution.

Potential Roadblock #2: Communication Breakdowns.

Despite best efforts, communication with your ex-spouse may deteriorate.

Prevention:

- Reiterate Commitment to Respectful Communication: Remind yourself and your ex-spouse of your shared commitment to respectful dialogue. This is outlined in your co-parenting agreement.
- Utilize Written Communication: If verbal communication becomes strained, transition to written communication. Utilize email or text messaging. Maintain a neutral and objective tone.

- Seek Professional Assistance: If communication breakdowns persist, consult with a therapist or counselor. They can provide strategies for improving communication.

Potential Roadblock #3: Introduction of New Romantic Partners.

The introduction of new partners into the existing family structure can often create significant tension and complicate the already delicate co-parenting dynamic that has been established.

Prevention:

- Establish Guidelines in Co-Parenting Agreement: Address the issue of new partners in your co-parenting agreement. Outline a process for introductions and communication.

- Prioritize Gradual Integration: Introduce new partners to your children gradually. Ensure they understand the importance of respecting the established co-parenting relationship.
- Maintain Open Communication: Discuss concerns with your ex-spouse regarding new partners. Do this in a respectful and constructive manner.

Remember, the objective is not to eliminate all conflict. It is to manage disagreements constructively. Do this while prioritizing the best interests of your children. By anticipating potential challenges and employing these preventative measures, you can maintain a functional co-parenting relationship.

Section 5: Troubleshooting - Addressing Common Co-Parenting Concerns

Here are some frequently asked questions regarding Deliberate Dissolution and co-parenting, addressed from a legal perspective:

Q: What are the most common challenges parents face while co-parenting during the divorce process?

A: During divorce proceedings, parents often encounter several significant challenges in co-parenting:

1. High levels of conflict: Disagreements over parenting styles, rules, and routines are common and can be detrimental to children's emotional well-being
2. Communication breakdowns: Effective communication is crucial but often suffers due to lingering resentment or emotional distress.
3. Manipulation and control attempts: Some parents may try to use the child as a means of control over the other parent or attempt to alienate the child from the other parent

4. Inconsistency in parenting: Maintaining consistent approaches and rules can be challenging when parents are not aligned.
5. Emotional impact on children: Children often experience a range of painful emotions during their parents' divorce, which can be exacerbated by ongoing parental conflict.
6. Legal and custodial disputes: Battles over custody and visitation rights can be stressful and contentious, prolonging the divorce process

As an attorney, I strongly advise parents to prioritize their children's well-being and work towards a cooperative co-parenting relationship, even during the challenging divorce process. Seeking the assistance of a mediator or therapist can be beneficial in managing conflict and improving communication.

Q: How can parents maintain effective communication during and after divorce?

A: Maintaining effective communication is crucial for successful co-parenting. As an attorney, I recommend the following strategies:

1. Use neutral, business-like language in all communications.
2. Stick to child-related topics and avoid discussing personal matters or past relationship issues.
3. Utilize written communication methods (e.g., email, text messages, or co-parenting apps) to maintain a record of discussions and agreements.
4. Respond to the other parent's communications promptly and respectfully.
5. Keep each other informed about important matters concerning the children, such as school events or medical appointments
6. Consider using a mediator or parenting coordinator if direct communication proves consistently difficult.

Remember, effective communication is not only beneficial for your co-parenting relationship but is often viewed favorably by courts in custody matters.

Q: What legal issues might arise in co-parenting after the divorce is finalized?

A: Even after a divorce is finalized, several legal issues can arise in co-parenting situations:

1. Modifications to custody arrangements: Changes in circumstances (e.g., relocation, job changes) may necessitate adjustments to existing custody agreements
2. Enforcement of custody orders: If one parent consistently violates the custody agreement, legal action may be required to enforce the order.
3. Child support disputes: Disagreements over payment amounts, timing, or additional expenses can lead to legal conflicts.
4. Decision-making conflicts: Major decisions regarding the child's education, health, or welfare may require legal intervention if parents cannot agree.

5. Parental alienation claims: If one parent believes the other is actively trying to damage their relationship with the child, they may seek legal recourse.
6. Contempt of court actions: Failure to adhere to court-ordered parenting plans can result in contempt proceedings.

As an attorney, I advise clients to document all instances of non-compliance with court orders and to attempt resolution through mediation before pursuing litigation. Courts generally favor arrangements that prioritize the child's best interests

Q: How can parents ensure consistency between households after divorce?

A: Ensuring consistency between households is crucial for children's stability. As an attorney, I recommend the following approaches:

1. Develop a detailed parenting plan: This should outline rules, routines, and expectations for both households.
2. Use a shared calendar: Implement a digital calendar to track schedules, appointments, and important events.
3. Maintain open communication: Regularly discuss any changes or issues that arise in either household.
4. Be flexible: Allow for some differences between households while maintaining core rules and values.
5. Consider using a parenting coordinator: This professional can help mediate disagreements and ensure consistency in parenting approaches.

6. Document agreements: Keep a record of any new agreements or modifications to the parenting plan.

Research shows that consistency between households can significantly reduce stress and confusion for children, leading to better adjustment post-divorce

Q: What are the legal implications of introducing new partners to children after divorce?

A: Introducing new partners to children after divorce can be a sensitive issue with potential legal implications:

1. Custody modifications: The introduction of a new partner could lead to requests for custody modifications if one parent believes it negatively impacts the child.
2. Right of first refusal: Some custody agreements include a "right of first refusal" clause, which may be triggered if a new partner is caring for the child during the other parent's designated time.
3. Morality clauses: Some divorce decrees include morality clauses that restrict overnight guests when children are present.
4. Child safety concerns: If there are legitimate concerns about a new partner's impact on the child's safety or well-being, this could lead to legal action.

5. Parental alienation claims: If the introduction of a new partner is handled poorly, it could potentially be used as evidence in parental alienation claims.

As an attorney, I advise clients to approach this situation carefully, giving children time to adjust to the divorce before introducing new partners. It's also crucial to review your custody agreement and consult with legal counsel before making significant changes to your living situation.

Q: How do courts view parental conflict in co-parenting situations?

A: Courts take parental conflict very seriously in co-parenting situations. Here's what you need to know:

1. Best interests of the child: Courts prioritize the child's best interests, which often means favoring arrangements that minimize conflict exposure.
2. Impact on custody decisions: High levels of parental conflict can influence custody decisions, potentially leading to reduced parenting time for the parent deemed more responsible for the conflict.
3. Mandatory mediation or counseling: Courts may order parents to attend mediation or counseling to address ongoing conflicts.
4. Parenting coordinators: In high-conflict cases, courts may appoint a parenting coordinator to help manage disputes and facilitate communication.

5. Modification of custody orders: Persistent, high-conflict situations may lead to modifications of existing custody orders to protect the child's well-being.
6. Consideration of children's preferences: In cases of high conflict, courts may give more weight to older children's preferences regarding custody arrangements.

Recent studies have shown that high levels of interparental conflict can lead to behavioral and emotional problems in children. As an attorney, I strongly advise clients to manage their disputes away from their children and to prioritize cooperative co-parenting to avoid negative legal consequences and, more importantly, to protect their children's well-being.

Q: What legal resources are available to help with co-parenting challenges?

A: There are several legal resources available to assist with co-parenting challenges:

1. Parenting Act guidelines: Many states provide detailed guidelines for creating effective parenting plans
2. Court-appointed Guardians ad Litem (GAL): These professionals represent the child's best interests in custody disputes.
3. Custody and parenting time investigation services: Court investigators can provide recommendations regarding custody and parenting time
4. Mediation services: Many courts offer or mandate mediation services for co-parenting disputes.
5. Parenting coordinators: These professionals can be appointed to help manage ongoing co-parenting conflicts.

6. Legal aid organizations: These can provide free or low-cost legal assistance for co-parenting issues.
7. Online legal resources: Many state court websites offer forms, guidelines, and information specific to co-parenting and custody issues.

As an attorney, I recommend utilizing these resources to help navigate co-parenting challenges. They can provide valuable guidance and support, often at a lower cost than traditional litigation. Remember, while these resources are helpful, they should not replace personalized legal advice. Always consult with a qualified family law attorney for guidance on your specific situation.

Q: What if my ex-spouse refuses to cooperate or participate in Deliberate Dissolution?

A: While mutual cooperation is ideal, you can still implement the principles of Deliberate Dissolution unilaterally. Focus on your own behavior and adhere to the terms of your co-parenting agreement. Document any instances of non-cooperation. Consult with your attorney regarding potential legal remedies.

Q: How do we address holidays and special occasions in our co-parenting agreement?

A: Your co-parenting agreement should include a detailed schedule for holidays and special occasions. This should take into account the children's preferences and the logistical constraints of both parents. Strive for equitable division of time. Be prepared to compromise.

Q: What if my child is experiencing emotional difficulties as a result of the divorce?

A: It is not uncommon for children to experience emotional challenges during and after divorce. Monitor your children's behavior closely. Seek professional help from a child psychologist or therapist if needed. They can provide support and guidance.

Q: How do we make decisions regarding our children's education, healthcare, and extracurricular activities?

A: Your co-parenting agreement should specify the process for making these decisions. If you have joint legal custody, you must strive to make these decisions jointly. If disagreements arise, consult with a mediator or your respective attorneys.

Q: How long does it take to establish a stable and functional co-parenting relationship?

A: Establishing a stable co-parenting relationship is an ongoing process. It requires consistent effort and a commitment to the principles of Deliberate Dissolution. There is no fixed timeline. Be patient and persistent.

Section 6: Conclusion - Securing a Positive Future for Your Family

This guide has provided a legal framework for Deliberate Dissolution. It has outlined the steps necessary to navigate divorce in a manner that prioritizes your children's well-being. By implementing this process, you can establish a foundation for a successful co-parenting relationship. This will minimize conflict and promote a stable environment for your children.

The benefits of this approach are numerous:

- Reduced Litigation: A collaborative approach minimizes the need for costly and adversarial court battles.
- Child-Centric Outcomes: Prioritizing the best interests of the child leads to more favorable outcomes for their emotional and psychological well-being.
- Empowerment: This process empowers you to take control of your post-divorce life and create a positive future for your family.
- Preservation of Parental Rights: Deliberate Dissolution helps ensure that both parents remain actively involved in their children's lives. This upholds their legal rights and responsibilities.

The path to Deliberate Dissolution requires diligence and a steadfast commitment to your children's welfare. It may present challenges. However, the rewards of a successful co-parenting relationship are immeasurable.

Take action now. Initiate a dialogue with your ex-spouse about adopting this approach. Begin drafting your co-parenting agreement. Consult with legal and mental health professionals as needed.

By embracing Deliberate Dissolution, you are choosing a path that prioritizes your children's needs. You are laying the groundwork for a more harmonious future. This is a future where your children can thrive despite the changes in your family structure. This is a legally sound approach. It is an approach that fosters cooperation, minimizes conflict, and safeguards the well-being of your children. This is the path to a new beginning, defined not by the dissolution of your marriage, but by the strength and resilience of your family.

Things to think about

Feel free to write down any after-reading insights and thoughts

After reading this, I feel right now...

1. ______________________________
2. ______________________________
3. ______________________________
4. ______________________________
5. ______________________________
6. ______________________________
7. ______________________________
8. ______________________________
9. ______________________________
10. ______________________________

Weekly planner

Plan and manage your weekly tasks. Simply reference the page number you want to work on for each day.

	Monda y	Tuesd ay	Wedn esday	Thurs day	Friday	Satur day	Sunda y
1							
2							
3							
4							
5							
6							

Andy Patzig is an attorney licensed in both Virginia and Washington D.C.. For over a decade Andy has been practicing almost exclusively in family law which includes divorce, custody, visitation, support, and also abuse and neglect. As a Guardian ad litem in Virginia, Andy has been involved in over 500 cases involving children.

In addition to his work as an attorney, Andy is also a licensed Realtor in Virginia, a GAL, a trained mediator, a certified divorce coach, and an overall helpful guy. This book is not the product of arrogance but an attempt to help people achieve a more satisfying resolution to their family law issues.

Andy Patzig, Esq.

www.ingramcontent.com/pod-product-compliance
Lightning Source LLC
La Vergne TN
LVHW022224200926
848481LV00006B/2109